6 RMS RIV VU

A COMEDY BY
BOB RANDALL

NELSON DOUBLEDAY, INC.
GARDEN CITY, NEW YORK

6 RMS RIV VU was first presented
at the Helen Hayes Theatre,
New York, October 17, 1972.

Produced by Alexander H. Cohen and Bernard Delfont
Directed by Edwin Sherin
Scenery by William Ritman
Costumes by Ann Roth
Lighting by Marc B. Weiss

THE CAST
(in order of appearance)

EDDIE, the Superintendent — Jose Ocasio

THE PREGNANT WOMAN — Anna Shaler

LARRY, her Husband — F. Murray Abraham

ANNE MILLER — Jane Alexander

PAUL FRIEDMAN — Jerry Orbach

THE WOMAN IN 4A — Francine Beers

JANET FRIEDMAN — Jennifer Warren

RICHARD MILLER — Ron Harper

Synopsis of Scenes

An empty Riverside Drive apartment.
The time is the present

ACT ONE
  Scene 1: Late morning
  Scene 2: Eight o'clock that night

ACT TWO
  The next morning

ACT ONE

SCENE 1

The living room of a large rent-controlled apartment on Riverside Drive. The room is bare and in
need of painting. Two windows in the upstage wall
face out on a brick wall. Stage right is a doorway
that leads to the dining room, kitchen and maid's
room. In the upstage wall, far left, is a doorway that
leads to the bedrooms. On the stage left wall is the
entrance to the apartment up a few steps from the
apartment level.

The front door is missing its doorknob. The SUPER-
INTENDENT, EDDIE, opens it from off-stage, a door-
knob in his hand, and a YOUNG COUPLE dashes in.
She is quite pregnant and pushes a baby carriage.
They leave the carriage on the landing.

WOMAN

All right, check the bedrooms, closets and bathrooms. I'll take
the kitchen.

(He dashes into the bedrooms. She runs into the
dining room. EDDIE screws the doorknob into the
door and exits. The YOUNG COUPLE returns)

3

LARRY

Honey, the master's gigantic! Two walk-ins and there's a stall shower! But the second bedroom doesn't have a closet and the floor's pink.

WOMAN

Who cares! It's still rent-controlled. There's room for a sit-down table if we move the refrigerator. And, Larry, there's a half-bath in the maid's room.

LARRY

My darkroom!

(He kisses her with glee and exits into the dining room area to see it. She calls after him)

WOMAN

Hold your breath. There's something rotting behind the sink.

(The baby cries)

Cool it, Justin, Mommy's busy!

(She exits into the bedrooms while the baby continues to cry. In a moment, they return exultant)

LARRY

I'll bribe up to two thousand!

WOMAN

You'll have to.

LARRY

Thank God the landlord was caught harassing the last tenant.

WOMAN

Let's get down to the agent's. I'm going to get a highboy!

(She stops on the steps and surveys the apartment)

There's so many things I can do with this place.

LARRY

(Joining her after looking out the window)

If we could turn it around to face the river, it'd be perfect!

WOMAN

Knock it off, Justin!

(They dash out of the apartment with the baby carriage, he poking his head in for a last look and slamming the door. Pause. ANNE enters. She's in her early thirties, attractive. She has an air of mild exhaustion about her, as if she's taken time out from a busy day fighting with the kids and the super to run over and see the apartment. She keeps pot in a cookie canister, has a shelf filled with books on how you raise children and is getting a little bored. A satisfactory life, all in all. She looks out the window at the wall)

ANNE

So, how often do you look out the window?

(She begins to pace the room)

Three, six, nine, twelve, fifteen, eighteen, twenty-one, twenty-three.

(Starts again at other wall)

Three, six, nine, twelve, fifteen, eighteen, twenty. Twenty by twenty-three, could you die?

(Sings and exits into dining room)

Oh, give me room lots of room, under starry skies . . . *

---

* Portion of lyrics from "Don't Fence Me In", words and music by Cole Porter. © 1944 Harms Inc. Copyright renewed. All rights reserved. Used by permission of Warner Bros. Music.

5

(PAUL enters through the front door. He is her male counterpart, same age. He's a copywriter at an ad agency, on the Way Up and also a little bored. He looks around the room and out the window)

PAUL

Yucch!

(He exits into bedrooms. ANNE is heard singing off-stage. PAUL hears her and re-enters. ANNE enters, singing raucously)

ANNE

. . . let me be by myself in the evening breeze
List'ning to the murmur of the cottonwood trees
Send me out forever, but I ask you please
Don't fence me . . .

(She reacts violently as she sees PAUL)

PAUL

Sing it, baby.

ANNE

Excuse me.

PAUL

I'm sorry. I was just kidding.

(She exits into bedrooms)

Three, six, nine, twelve . . .

ANNE

(Re-enters)

It's twenty by twenty-three.

PAUL

Thanks.

ANNE

Look, I'm not one of your West Side schizophrenics.

PAUL

I didn't think you were.

ANNE

The apartment's so big, it got to me. I didn't know anybody else was in here.

PAUL

You don't have to explain.

ANNE

Ohh . . . did Schneider/Steinbrunner send you?

PAUL

Yeah.

ANNE

(Upset)

God! They told me they wouldn't send anybody else over today.

PAUL

Yeah, that's what they told me! Can you believe those two?
(Pause)
We've been looking for a bigger place for over a year.

ANNE

Next month is my second anniversary.

PAUL

We have a three and a half.

7

                    ANNE

We have one bedroom and an alcove.

                    PAUL

Any kids?

                    ANNE

Two.

                    PAUL

Relax. I'm only the envoy. My wife has the final say.

                    ANNE

Is she out of town, I hope? Go look at the dining room.

    (PAUL goes into the dining area, ANNE into the bed-
    room. EDDIE enters and exits with the trash basket,
    leaving the front door open)

    (PAUL and ANNE enter separately and examine the
    window again)

                    PAUL

Tell me, where's the river?

                    ANNE

If you lean out the second bathroom, it's to the left.

                    PAUL

    (Looking around)

Well, anyway, it's big.

                    ANNE

Yeah.

    8

PAUL

And a nice room, huh?

ANNE

I hate to admit it in front of you, but yes, it is. You put a couch over there and a few big overstuffed chairs here, by the window, facing *in* . . .

PAUL

My wife and I are more the caning and spindly-legs type.

ANNE

How eighteenth century of you.

PAUL

I like club chairs, but Janet doesn't. Do you have any club chairs at home?

ANNE

No, we have leather and chrome. My husband likes to sit up straight.

(She is peering into the closet by now)

PAUL

Not straighter than my wife. Hey, would you do me a favor? The second bedroom has no closet. I guess I could build one. Would you give me your opinion?

ANNE

Sure. My God, a strange man is inviting me into a bedroom. At last, something to tell the checker at the Daitch.

(They exit. EDDIE enters, eating a butter cookie and removes the doorknob and exits, slamming the door. ANNE and PAUL re-enter)

9

I never knew you could just build a closet. I thought it took an architect.

PAUL

Nothing to it. Do you like club chairs?

ANNE

Yes, I do.

PAUL

That's very significant. A woman who likes club chairs likes men.

ANNE

Erich Fromm?

PAUL

It's a man's chair. My father had a club chair.

ANNE

Everybody's did.

PAUL

What's a Morris chair?

ANNE

Search me. Look, I think I'd better get down to the agent's and wrestle with Eva Braun.

PAUL

Mrs. Schneider or Mrs. Steinbrunner?

ANNE

Schneider.

PAUL

(In a Nazi accent)

Und tell me, Madame, vhy do you vish to rent this apartment? Speak. Ve haff vays of making you talk.

ANNE

Notice their initials are S.S.

PAUL

Right. It's always nice to meet a fellow bigot. My name's Paul Friedman.

ANNE

Anne Miller.

PAUL

Really?

ANNE

You want to call Ripley?

PAUL

Didn't your parents go to the movies?

ANNE

They named me Delaney. The Miller was my husband's idea.

PAUL

My God, I just met Ann Miller. Hey, I'll ride down in the elevator with you.

(He reaches for the doorknob)

What happened here?

ANNE

Where's the doorknob?

PAUL

(After trying to open the door)

No use.

ANNE

(Banging on door)

Hello out there. We're stuck!

PAUL

(Looking out peephole)

There's nobody there.

(Calls)

Hello? Hello? This is 4B calling 4A.

(Beat)

They must be out.

ANNE

Hello, there's a young mother of two in distress in here!

PAUL

Is that how you see yourself? A young mother?

ANNE

When I want sympathy.

(Calls again)

Hello, there's a college-educated person locked in here! Better?

PAUL

Which college?

ANNE

Barnard.

PAUL

Did you know Beverly Strauss?

ANNE

Not well.

PAUL

Maybe they're walking the dog.

ANNE

(Calling into hole)

And I'm a dog lover!

(Beat)

You want to play Simon Says?

PAUL

Shall we try the window?

ANNE

Why not? I've always loved shrieking.

PAUL

Hey, Ma, throw me a nickel.

(He tries to open the window. It is stuck)

Would you lend me a hand?

13

ANNE

Sure.

PAUL

When I count three?

ANNE

On the three or four?

PAUL

What?

ANNE

One-two tug or one-two-three tug?

PAUL

Care for the extra count for preparation?

ANNE

Whatever you say.

PAUL

One-two-three tug.

ANNE

Roger.
    (They tug. Nothing happens)

PAUL

Once more. One-two-three tug!
    (Again nothing)

Wait a minute.

(He takes off his jacket, gets on his knees on the radiator and tries mightily to open it. Meanwhile, ANNE goes to the other window and opens it easily)

It's coming. It's coming.

(He opens it about an inch. Then he sees the other window)

Why didn't you tell me?

ANNE

I thought it might be a matter of machismo.

PAUL

(Good-naturedly)

You're a crazy lady.

(Indicating the open window)

Shall I?

ANNE

Please.

PAUL

Hello! Hello! There's a woman in the kitchen downstairs. Hello!

ANNE

Hello, miss! Madam!

PAUL

You! The lady in the half-slip! Damn, she ran out of the room.

15

ANNE

People of New York! There's a nice couple trapped in apartment 4B, six rooms, still rent-controlled, three twenty-five a month! Get us out and we'll give you the agent's name!

(Beat)

Do you think we'll come to hate each other after a few months?

PAUL

Permit a master.

(Calls out window)

Ladies and gentlemen, I see a parking space!

WOMAN'S VOICE

(Off-stage)

What?

(ANNE and PAUL look at each other)

ANNE

Genius.

PAUL

I was kidding, lady. We're locked in 4B. Somebody removed the doorknob and we . . .

(Off-stage can be heard the sound of a window slamming)

She slammed the window on me! How do you like that? She slammed the window!

ANNE

Well, you shouldn't kid about a thing like that.

PAUL

We *are* locked in.

ANNE

About the parking space.

PAUL

Yes, crazy lady. Help! Help! Soccoro, por favor! Of all the dumb things.

(ANNE wanders into the bedroom area while PAUL moves to the front door)

They let you in to see the apartment and then sneak the goddam doorknob out from under you. Suppose I had a ticket to the Knicks game? Suppose I had to go to the bathroom? The goddam toilets don't flush!

(ANNE has re-entered from the bedroom and starts to laugh)

What the hell is so funny?

ANNE

The service door.

PAUL

(Beat, smiles)

The service door. Of course. Who ever heard of a six-room apartment without a service door.

(They cross toward the dining room. PAUL stops at the windows and yells out)

Screw you, lady!

(To ANNE)

Shall we dance?

(They happily shuffle off-stage. A beat. They return
—downcast)

What kind of person would seal a service door permanently
shut?

ANNE

Probably an old lady who was afraid of burglars.
(A pause)

PAUL
(Moves to the windows)

What about your kids? Aren't you worried about them?

ANNE

The worst my mother can do is make them a little neurotic.
(A beat. After thinking that one over she moves
quickly to the door)

That did it. Help!

PAUL
(Sitting on the radiator)
Who'd steal a doorknob?

ANNE
(Banging on the front door)

Help!! Help!! Help!!
(A beat. She turns away)

Where did you go?

PAUL

N.Y.U.

ANNE

What class?

PAUL

'59.

ANNE

Did you know Stanley Counihan?

PAUL

I used to date his sister.

ANNE

(A squeal of delight)

She's my best friend!

PAUL

Oh, yeah. She was a crazy lady, too.

ANNE

Thanks.

PAUL

You know, for a while there, I think she really thought she was Elaine May.

ANNE

Unh-unh. She was Mike Nichols. *I* was Elaine May.

PAUL

You *are* crazy.

(Pause)

I mean that in the nicest possible way.

ANNE

What *is* the nicest possible way?

PAUL

It's all right. I'm crazy, too.

ANNE

You're just saying that to be kind.

PAUL

No. I can prove it.

ANNE

Go ahead.

PAUL

All right. In my closet, way in the back, in a little box, I have a Polaroid snapshot of Mamie Van Doren on the steps of the Astor Hotel, three hundred and fifty-four Adlai Stevenson buttons, Mort Sahl's autograph on a coaster from the Blue Angel, and, the pièce de résistance of my collection, all the Wonder Woman comic books from 1948 to 1952. Crazy?

ANNE

Amateur. I have a Katy Keene date-book.

PAUL

You're kidding.

ANNE

Every once in a while I lock myself in the john and read it.

PAUL

All about your old boy friends?

ANNE

No. Mostly my old sweater sets.
(A beat. She crosses down right)

You want to tell me your life story?

PAUL

All right. Did you know Karen Burke?

ANNE

She was a loose girl.

PAUL

Yeah. I once dated her.

ANNE

(Delighted)

Yes?

PAUL

She let me kiss her sweater set.

ANNE

(As if shocked)

Please! I only have two children.

PAUL

I wonder whatever became of Karen Burke.

ANNE

She married an analyst, has two kids and bought a nine-room co-op for sixty-five thousand.

PAUL

I always knew she'd end up bad.

ANNE

Hey, you're funny.

PAUL

Hey, so are you.

(They make eye contact, get nervous, a moment's awkward silence)

ANNE

(In a very tiny voice)

Help.

(A beat. He crosses to the door, she sits on the radiator)

What do you do?

PAUL

When I'm not hanging around empty apartments, I'm a copywriter.

ANNE

For what?

PAUL

Oh, a lot of crap. Soap, toothpaste, soft drinks.

22

SCENE 1 — *Act One*

ANNE

You don't like it, huh?

PAUL

Nope.

ANNE

What do you want to do?

PAUL

Retire.

ANNE

Seriously.

PAUL

Nothing. What do you want me to do?

ANNE

Don't you want to write a book?

PAUL

Nope.

ANNE

I thought all copywriters want to write a book.

PAUL

Wrong. Most of them want to write copy.

ANNE

And you don't?

23

PAUL

Right.

(He gives a small laugh at himself)

ANNE

Don't you want to do anything?

PAUL

Not in particular.

ANNE

I guess you *are* crazy.

PAUL

No more so than the rest of our do-nothing generation.

(He crosses down off the platform and moves toward her)

We're all dying of inertia. What about you?

(He leans against the arch, looking down at her)

What do you do?

ANNE

When I'm not in the john reading *Cashmere Confidential* I watch my children grow. And I copy edit a little.

PAUL

Oh, you were an editor before?

ANNE

In my previous life.

PAUL

Did you like it?

ANNE

Uh-huh. I once had lunch with John Updike.

PAUL

And now?

ANNE

Now I have lunch with my kids. Look, are you trying to de-
press me?

> (PAUL feels he has made a point. He pushes himself
> away from the arch and steps toward her)

PAUL

See what I mean about our generation?

ANNE

Yeah, but it happens in every generation. You have kids and
they come first.

> (A beat)

You know what I spend my days doing? Sorting socks. True.
Every once in a while I run across a stray argyle in the base-
ment dryer, but other than that . . .

PAUL

No, not every generation. I bet your mother was never bored.

ANNE

She was too busy cleaning linoleum.

PAUL

You know why?

25

ANNE

We had a lot of linoleum.

PAUL

Because she had something vital and important in her life. Something that kept her young and alive.

ANNE

My mother? What?

PAUL

The Depression.

ANNE

I think I missed a sentence.

PAUL

It gave her something to look forward to. Something to out-live.

(He turns away)

A great day's coming tomorrow. Happy days are here again. Today, what do we have?

(Turns back)

Nothing.

(Beginning to move)

We've lost our sense of life. Our struggle. Our parents had it. They fought to survive. The kids today have it. They're fighting to change the world.

(His voice rises)

What does our generation do? Peddle toothpaste and sort socks! If we disappeared from the face of the earth this minute, nobody'd know until our subscriptions to *New York* magazine ran out!

(At full steam)

No wonder we're bored to death!

ANNE

Did you take the doorknob?

PAUL

Bored! Bored! Bored!

ANNE

Not right now. Right now I'm a little nervous, nervous, nervous. Look, I'm a lot better at superficial talk.

(Crosses to the front door)

I think I'll try another plea for help.

PAUL

I'm sorry.

ANNE

It's okay.

(Bangs on the door)

HELP!

PAUL

I didn't mean to yell. I'm sorry.

ANNE

Forget it.

27

PAUL

That's just my way. I get excited. You ought to hear me scream at long traffic lights. I even cry for the ladies on TV whose wash isn't white enough.

(Beat)

Okay?

ANNE

(Turning back from the door)

Okay. At least I wasn't bored.

(She stamps on the floor with both feet as if trying to rouse the neighbors below. PAUL watches her, then imitates her stomping, but turns it into a parody of a Spanish fandango. He smiles at her, she smiles in return)

Won't your wife come looking for you soon?

PAUL

No, she's busy planning a women's lib dinner for tonight. What about your husband?

ANNE

Out of town on business. Women's lib, huh?

PAUL

Yes ma'am, or should I say "sir"?

ANNE

I wanted to get involved with women's lib, but then I signed up for pollution. Jerry Kretchmer's cute.

PAUL

There's nothing cute about some of the girls Janet brings home. When they're around I get the feeling I'd better fluff up the pillows or empty the ashtrays quick.

ANNE

Sexist.

PAUL

You wouldn't be happy in women's lib.

ANNE

(Sensing his animosity toward the Movement, her response is defiant)

Why not?

PAUL

(Backing down)

I'm only kidding. It's a very important movement. You ought to get involved in it.

ANNE

Now you sound like my analyst.

PAUL

Who do you go to?

ANNE

Charlie Berg, West Eighty-third. You?

PAUL

Jack Del Pesce, East Seventy-seventh.

29

ANNE

This is too much!

PAUL

What? You know Jack?

ANNE

He's my analyst's analyst. Boy, if you were a woman, I'd even know which hairdresser you went to.

PAUL

Clay.

ANNE

Right . . . what?

PAUL

Janet goes to him.

ANNE

How come I've never met you before, like in my shower, or someplace.

(Hears herself and turns, embarrassed)

You ought to meet my husband, Richard. You'd like each other.

PAUL

Does he go to a shrink, too?

ANNE

No, he's a WASP.

30

PAUL

Oh, I forgot. He sits on straight-back chairs.

ANNE

So does your wife, Janet.

PAUL

Oh, yeah. She does. Janet went to Smith. Ruined her for life.
You'd like her.

ANNE

You'd like Richard. Maybe if we ever get rescued we can all
meet at the Great Shanghai sometime.

(They are both sitting, he on the radiator, she on
the steps)

PAUL

Janet doesn't like Chinese food.

ANNE

Neither does Richard.

PAUL

I love their beef in oyster sauce.

ANNE

Beef with broccoli.

(They ad-lib Chinese dishes they like)

PAUL

(With regret)

Janet loves pizza. Boy, you ought to see her demolish a pie.

31

                    ANNE

Richard's crazy about potato pancakes.

                    PAUL

That's very liberal of him.

                    ANNE

I hate pizza.

                    PAUL

Me, too.

                    ANNE

Janet sounds very nice.

                    PAUL

So does Richard.

    (He suddenly jumps up)

Somebody's in the hall!

    (They run to the door and peer through peephole
    and latch hole)

She *was* walking the dog! Lady! Lady! 4A! Over here, in 4B!

                    WOMAN

Who's that?

                    PAUL

We're locked in here. Tell the super.

                    WOMAN

Where? Where are you?

ANNE

In 4B. We're locked in!

WOMAN

You're not supposed to be in there. That apartment is vacant.

PAUL

I know. We were looking at the apartment and somebody took the doorknob off. We can't get out.

(Reacting to what he sees)

For crissakes, she's opening her door! Lady! We can't get out! Tell the super!

WOMAN

You're not supposed to be in this building. You don't live here.

PAUL

Lady, the agent sent us to look at the apartment. Don't worry, we're respectable people.

WOMAN

I'm not getting involved.

ANNE

Please!

WOMAN

Who's in there with you?

ANNE

My name's Anne Miller.

WOMAN

The movie star? What are you, kidding around?

ANNE

No, not that Ann Miller. I'm a young mother of two and I work for pollution.

PAUL

Will you let me handle this?

WOMAN

You work for pollution? You think that's funny?

PAUL

I promise you we're nice people. I'm a businessman and she has two small children.

WOMAN

If she has two small children, why isn't she home taking care of them?

ANNE

Because the agent sent me over to see the apartment!

(Raising her hands in prayer)

God, will You interpret down here?

WOMAN

Stand away from the door. I'll take a look at you.

PAUL

Thanks.

(He takes ANNE by the hand and they move back into the room)

WOMAN

Get far away from the door! I can't see you.

PAUL

Okay, okay.

(They move back and stand at attention, smiling widely, trying to look respectable)

Hello.

ANNE

How do you do. It's a very nice building. You must have a lovely apartment.

WOMAN

What do you care about my apartment?

ANNE

I just meant you're lucky to live in such a nice building.

WOMAN

A lot you know.

PAUL

That's a nice dog you've got there.

ANNE

We have a dog. A schnauzer. What kind is yours?

WOMAN

A Doberman pinscher. I suppose you're all right. At least you cut your hair.

35

ANNE

Oh yes, we both cut our hair all the time. I'm going to cut mine even shorter. I hate long hair. Don't you hate long hair, Paul? He does.

PAUL

(Still grinning)

Will you tell the super?

WOMAN

If I could find the super, I'd tell him to fix my sink.

PAUL

Please, lady!

ANNE

Lady, I've got to get out of here. My kids are waiting for me.
(Beat)
Lady?
(Beat)
Nice lady?
(Beat)
Doberman pinscher lady?
(They break ranks and run to the door)

PAUL

(Looking out)

She went into her apartment!

ANNE

Can you resist this place? I think I'll throw myself out the window. With any luck I'll just break my legs and I can crawl to the street for help.

PAUL

Don't bother. Who's going to go near a lady crawling down Riverside Drive?

ANNE

You're right.
> (They wander about in frustration. Finally she stretches out on the radiator, PAUL sits on platform steps)

Where were we? Oh, yeah. You were telling me about Janet.

PAUL

Yeah, you'd like her.

ANNE

You'd like Richard.

PAUL

Goddam it, if Janet wasn't fixing dinner for that group of hers, I wouldn't have had to come here in the first place.

ANNE

> (Not liking the idea)

And I'd be stuck here with her.

PAUL

> (Almost an order)

You'd like her!

37

ANNE

All right.

PAUL

Well, you think *I* want to be locked up with a guy who'd stand around at attention the whole time?

ANNE

What's the matter with you?

PAUL

Nothing. But nobody has to get *stuck* with my wife except me!

ANNE

(Beat)

Richard would have gotten us out of here by now.

PAUL

And Janet wouldn't have chased that woman away by saying every dumb thing that came into her head.

ANNE

My name *is* Anne Miller!

PAUL

Who asked you? If my name was Count Dracula, I wouldn't tell everybody I met in a dark alley.

ANNE

I think you must be cranky because you don't have any nice soft club chairs to sink into!

PAUL

And I think you've been sorting too many socks lately!

ANNE

(After a frozen silence)

I see no need for our talking to each other. Why don't we make this confinement solitary?

PAUL

That suits me fine. I'll sit in the dining room.

(He stalks out of the room, his head averted from her. ANNE sits there, angry, then annoyed, then ashamed. She goes to the front door and looks out again. Then she turns and walks to the dining room archway)

ANNE

I'm sorry, Paul. I didn't mean to make a crack about your wife. I was just upset about the Wolf Woman, that's all.

(Silence)

Don't be that way. I said I'm sorry.

(Silence)

If you don't forgive me, I'm going to tell my analyst to tell your analyst.

(Silence)

Paul?

(She goes into the dining room)

Paul? Where are you? Don't leave me here alone!

(She comes out and rushes into the bedrooms)

Paul! Where did you go? Paul!!

(He comes running in from the dining room, she returns and they meet at center, grabbing for each other)

39

Where were you?

PAUL

I was in the maid's room. I was trying to signal to somebody across the courtyard. Look, I'm sorry.

ANNE

So am I. It was my fault. I'd be delighted to be stuck here with Janet.

PAUL

And I'd consider it a privilege to be locked up with Richard.

ANNE

Well, he *can* be a bit of a pain when things go wrong.

PAUL

And if Janet were here you really would have thrown yourself out the window.

ANNE

You don't need to say that on my account.

PAUL

No, it's true. She can make complaining an art form.

ANNE

Richard would have punched you in the nose by now. I'm glad he's not here.

PAUL

I'm glad Janet's not.
(Beat)
That sounds terrible, doesn't it?

ANNE

A little.

PAUL

Funny, the things you hear yourself say. I'm not usually a disloyal type. When the guys at the office make cracks about their wives, I always feel crummy about it. I never do that.

ANNE

Neither do I.

PAUL

It's not that every once in a while I wouldn't like to. Just to . . . get even . . . like after a fight. But I'd feel so . . . disloyal, you know?

ANNE

I know.

PAUL

Not that it would hurt Janet. She wouldn't know about it.

ANNE

True.

PAUL

I mean, how loyal can you be, right?

ANNE

Right.

PAUL

Right.

41

ANNE

(Pause. Swept up in a fantasy of "getting even."
Smiling naughtily)

Richard has sagging pectorals.

PAUL

What?

ANNE

(Indicating her chest)

Sagging pectorals. Here.

PAUL

Oh.

ANNE

He always wears an undershirt because he doesn't want us to
see his sagging pectorals.

PAUL

Sagging pectorals, wow.

ANNE

(Suddenly catching herself)

I shouldn't have told you.

PAUL

No, that's all right. You weren't being disloyal.

ANNE

(Upset)

Yes, I was. Oh God, was I ever!

PAUL

I don't think so. If I had sagging pectorals, I wouldn't mind Janet mentioning it in passing.

ANNE

I didn't mention it in passing. I drove out of my way to get there. And if Janet told, you'd mind.

PAUL

No, I wouldn't. Not any more than Janet would mind my telling she has a beard.

(Beat)

A little one.

ANNE

I have a feeling being locked up is having an adverse effect on our characters.

PAUL

I do feel strange.

ANNE

So do I. You know what it is?

PAUL

What?

ANNE

I haven't been really alone with a man other than Richard in about seven years.

PAUL

Hey, that's true. That's weird.

43

ANNE

Except the man who does the windows. And the super.

PAUL

Sometimes I'm alone with my secretary, but she doesn't count. She's a vegetable. It's spooky, you know? But I like it.

ANNE

Yeah. So do I. It feels wicked.

PAUL

No. You know what it really feels?

ANNE

What?

PAUL

Young. When's the last time you felt young?

ANNE

I think Grover Cleveland was in office.

PAUL

Right. It's the damn postwar baby boom. It's all their fault.

ANNE

Oh, good. Give me someone to blame.

PAUL

Well, it's true. I mean, there we were in our mid-twenties, barely polishing up our twist . . .

ANNE

(Twisting)

44

God love you, Chubby Checker, wherever you are.

PAUL

. . . and then one day we turn around and the whole damn
world is full of teenagers. Millions of them wherever you look.
And it's not so bad that they're younger than we are, they have
to be so damn different. They set up that generation gap and
pushed us on the other side with the grown-ups. I never chose
to be a grown-up, but it was too late. I'd already thrown away
my faded levis.

ANNE

My downfall was the day I first went to the beauty parlor.

PAUL

Right. Next thing you know we'll be shopping for burial plots.

ANNE

When I die I want to be pushed under the sink.

PAUL

Damn.

ANNE

Don't feel bad. For an older man I think you're awfully nice.

PAUL

Thank you. I think you're a knockout.

ANNE

You shouldn't say that.

PAUL

I'm sorry.

45

ANNE

(Beat)

You do?

PAUL

Yes, I really do.

ANNE

In what way am I a knockout?

PAUL

Well, you're one hell of a good sport for openers. And you're pretty. And you're fun. And you're a smart cookie . . .

ANNE

All right, stop. I always used to be a smart cookie, before I was married. I didn't know I still was.

PAUL

Sure you are.

ANNE

I was the office Eve Arden.

PAUL

I like a quick wit.

ANNE

You can't be very witty with the diaper man.

PAUL

(Sympathetically)

No.

46

ANNE

In college I was a beatnik. Isn't that a beautiful word? "Beat
. . . nik"? I never said a thing that wasn't a non sequitur. God,
I thought I was Zelda Fitzgerald.

PAUL

I was J. D. Salinger.

ANNE

Even when I met my husband it was straight out of Fitzgerald.
He was on the beach at Sag Harbor reading *Atlas Shrugged*
and I asked him if he'd read *The Fountainhead* and he
asked me if I'd read *Raise High the Roofbeam, Carpenters* and
I said I had and he said he had so we went to bed together.

PAUL

Janet and I met at a party. We were on the same charades
team. I guessed all hers and she guessed all mine . . .

ANNE

So you went to bed together.

PAUL

We finished the game first.

ANNE

Funny how in those days if you went to bed together you got
married. Boy, that feels like a million years ago. Thanks, Paul,
for making me feel like Zelda Fitzgerald again.

PAUL

You shouldn't lose her. She's a terrific girl.

47

ANNE

Tell you what I'll do. Tonight, when Richard calls in, I'll hit him with a few non sequiturs, just to keep in practice.

(Pause)

PAUL

(With apparent difficulty)

Listen, you're not doing anything special tonight and Janet's tied up with her mob, so why don't we have dinner tonight?

ANNE

What?

PAUL

Dinner. Together.

ANNE

Oh, I can't.

PAUL

Why not?

ANNE

I just can't.

PAUL

Sure you can.

ANNE

I'd feel funny. I even feel funny now that you asked me.

PAUL

So do I. Believe it or not, I've never asked another woman out before, since Janet.

ANNE

I believe it. You're not the type.

PAUL

Then have dinner with me.

ANNE

Paul . . .

PAUL

Come on. We make each other feel good. Come on, it'll help you get through tomorrow's linoleum. What's the harm?

ANNE

Paul, you know we're not the kind of people who do things like that.

PAUL

Like what? Eat? All I'm asking you for is dinner.

ANNE

I don't even know you!

PAUL

Of course you know me. I'm the guy who went out with all your girl friends at Barnard and uses your hairdresser and goes to your analyst's analyst. Even my mother doesn't know me that well.

ANNE

Then have dinner with your mother and let her find out.

PAUL

My mother doesn't make me feel good.

49

ANNE

It's not that I wouldn't like to . . . I've seen tonight's nine o'clock movie . . . I know there's no harm in it, it's just dinner . . . but I couldn't. I would feel so . . . illicit.

PAUL

We'll go Dutch treat. What's illicit about paying for yourself?

ANNE

I couldn't, really.

PAUL

Then I'll treat.

ANNE

No . . . where would we go?

PAUL

The Great Shanghai.

ANNE

I couldn't. All our friends go there.

PAUL

Oh. Ours, too.

ANNE

Not that there's anything wrong with them seeing us, it's just how would I explain it?

PAUL

You're right. What about Stark's? No, Janet's mother hangs out there.

ANNE

Tibb's Wharf?

PAUL

If Janet's mother isn't at Stark's, she'll be at Tibb's Wharf.

(The front door opens and EDDIE enters)

EDDIE

Mrs. Weiss said you were stuck in here.

PAUL

In a minute. How about . . .

ANNE

Paul!

PAUL

(Realizing it)

Hey! 4A sent help.

EDDIE

Not her.

(Pointing at window)

Across the court. Sorry, I didn't know you were in here when I took off the doorknob. I do that to keep people out. I'll leave it on and you and the missus can leave whenever you're ready.

(He waits for a tip, jingling change in his pocket as a prompting, then leaves when PAUL fails to pick up on it)

51

ANNE

Well, once again . . .

PAUL

I know! Let's have a picnic!

ANNE

(Gathers her belongings)

It's supposed to rain tonight.

PAUL

We'll have it here!

ANNE

Here?

PAUL

Sure! The apartment's empty. Why not?

ANNE

Oh, listen, let's just stop this before we're both sorry.

PAUL

I don't want to stop it. I want to have dinner with you. A perfectly straightforward, aboveboard, respectable dinner between two friends.

ANNE

In an empty apartment?

PAUL

Don't be so middle class.

52

ANNE

That's middle class? Not to have dinner with a strange man in an empty apartment? No, no, no.

PAUL

Now you're being silly.

ANNE

I suppose I am, but it's the only way I can be.

PAUL

I wish you'd change your mind.

ANNE

(Extends her hand)

It was really terrific meeting you, Paul. Goodbye.

PAUL

(Takes her hand)

Damn it, I'm not taking no for an answer. I'll be here at seven-thirty with a full picnic basket.

ANNE

I'm not coming, Paul.

PAUL

I'll be here anyway.

ANNE

(Taking her hand from his and going to door)

You'll be wasting an evening.

53

PAUL

I'd have to lock myself in the bedroom at home anyway. Look, I'll bring some Wonder Woman comic books with me. How can you resist that?

ANNE

(Turning at the door)

Ciao.

PAUL

Seven-thirty.

(ANNE smiles and exits.

PAUL stands looking after her for a moment, then starts to turn to get his coat. ANNE comes back, just inside the doorway)

ANNE

I can't make it before eight.

(ANNE exits. PAUL smiles, puts on his coat, begins to wonder what he's gotten himself into, then starts out)

CURTAIN

SCENE 2

The apartment is dark. Thunder is heard. The front door opens and in the hall light we can see ANNE standing there, dressed in a raincoat. She checks the doorknob. She calls inside.

ANNE

Paul? Are you in there?

(She checks her watch)

Eight o'clock. Ready or not, here I come.

(She takes a small step into the room)

Paul?

(She feels around the wall for the light switch and turns on the overhead light. She comes into the room, goes to the bedroom hall and turns on the light switch there)

All right, I'll start without him.

(She approaches the dining room nervously, tiptoes in quickly and turns on the lights, then returns to the living room. She paces the room)

Three, six, nine, twelve, fifteen, eighteen, twenty-one, twenty-three. You haven't changed a bit. What am I doing here, meeting a man I hardly know for a picnic on the floor of an empty rent-controlled apartment? Dear Rose Franzblau, my problem is this . . .

55

(ANNE starts to leave, gets to the front door where she hears PAUL coming from the elevator. She rushes back into the room and does a little "twist" step as she goes which causes her skirt to fall to its full length, revealing the long gown she has worn for the occasion. PAUL appears in the doorway laden down with three shopping bags and a smaller brown paper bag)

PAUL

I'm sorry I'm late, but the Hadassah was holding a buy-in at the A&P. You came.

ANNE

So did you. What on earth have you got there?

PAUL

(Kicks the door shut, takes off his coat and lays the bags down)

Supper.

ANNE

Is your wife's group joining us?

PAUL

No, thank God. When I last saw the ladies of liberation they were starting on their third pitcher of whiskey sours.

(He has by now taken five full paper bags out of one of the shopping bags)

ANNE

I have a riddle for you.

(Looking at the bags)

56

What comes in a hundred paper bags that two people could possibly eat in one sitting?

PAUL

(Spreading a blanket on the floor)

Yeah. I guess it's a little more than we need, but I didn't know what you liked.

ANNE

(Opening one of the bags)

Five apples? We going to bob?

PAUL

They were two pounds for forty-nine, so I got two pounds.

ANNE

(Opening another bag)

And two pounds of oranges?

PAUL

Also peaches, bananas and grapes.

ANNE

Ten pounds of fruit. Did somebody die?

(She takes off her coat and puts it on the radiator)

PAUL

(A beat, seeing her in the gown and appreciating it. He takes each item out of the bag as he describes it)

And for dessert. Sara Lee. You like barbecued chicken? If not, I got a pastrami on rye—and a rare roast beef—with Russian—

57

(ANNE sits on the blanket and PAUL is aware he is
in much more casual attire, then he continues taking
food out of the shopping bag. The bottle of wine is
in the separate small bag)

Also, caviar, red. Sorry about that. Fritos, plastic wine glasses,
bottle of wine, cole slaw, sweet peppers, plastic utensils, paper
plates, napkins in the mod boutique pattern, shocking pink
after dinner mints and a six-month supply of Wash 'n Dri.
Did I forget anything?

ANNE

A soufflé.

PAUL

(Goes to other shopping bag)

Yes, I did. Wonder Woman comics, I'm a man of my word.

(Takes out cassette player)

Music to dine by. I hope you like to eat by Chopin.

ANNE

I never heard To Eat by Chopin.

PAUL

We'll ignore that, shall we?

(She has emptied the small bags of their fruit onto
the blanket)

And the final touch.

(From the third shopping bag he takes out two
inflatable plastic chairs and a hand pump)

Club chairs.

ANNE

I was afraid you'd try to make a pass at me. By the time you
blow those things up you'll be lucky if you can shake my hand.

PAUL

Says you.
(Pumping)
Were you really afraid I'd make a pass?

ANNE

A little.

PAUL

So was I.

ANNE

Is that everything?

PAUL

Practically.

ANNE

What else?

PAUL

I'm not so sure I want to tell you.

ANNE

Why?

PAUL

I want to see how the evening goes first.

59

ANNE

Come on, Paul, tell me.

PAUL

Guess.

ANNE

A Monopoly set.

PAUL

Oh, damn it, do you like Monopoly, too?

ANNE

No!

PAUL

Oh. Well, I'm glad I didn't bring one.

ANNE

A TV set?

PAUL

Nope. You said you'd seen the nine o'clock movie.

ANNE

I know. You brought your college yearbook.

PAUL

(Pointing to food)

Go ahead, eat.

ANNE

Tell me. What did you bring?

60

PAUL

(Sheepishly taking it out of the bag)

My college yearbook.

ANNE

(Laughing)

Let's see.

(Opens it and flips through the pages)

Friedman . . . Friedman . . . hey, you were cute.

PAUL

(Pumping again)

You're looking at Arthur Friedman. Turn the page.

ANNE

(Does so)

Oh no, is that you? I didn't know you were hydrocephalic.

PAUL

Never take a crew cut if you've got a high forehead.

ANNE

I'll remember.

(She laughs again at the picture)

PAUL

I developed late.

ANNE

From what?

PAUL

It's easy for you to talk, Mrs. Miller. We don't have your yearbook here.

ANNE

Some of us are smart. I'm sorry. You were very . . . interesting-looking.

(She laughs again)

PAUL

Just read under my picture, that's all, smart ass.

ANNE

Paul Friedman. President of the Art and Literary Society, I am impressed, treasurer of the Junior Prom, member of the Little Theatre Honor Society, be still my heart . . .

PAUL

Yes, ma'am. I played Gaylord Ravenal in *Show Boat.*

ANNE

So did I! In girl's camp!

PAUL

I don't believe you.

ANNE

(Sings)

You are love
Here in my arms, where you belong . . . *

* Portion of lyrics from "You Are Love" by Jerome Kern and Oscar Hammerstein II. Copyright 1927 T. B. Harms Company. Copyright renewed. Used by permission.

PAUL

(Singing)

And here you will stay
I'll not let you away . . .

BOTH

I want day after day . . .

ANNE

(PAUL stops to hear her baritone)

. . . with you.

PAUL

(Still pumping)

I think you made a better Gaylord Ravenal than I did.

ANNE

Well, I was probably taller anyway.
    (Watching him)

You're going to develop quite a bust line.

PAUL

(Pumping even harder)

You ought to get Richard to try this.

ANNE

T'ain't funny, McGee.

PAUL

I'm sorry.

63

(He has finished inflating the chair and now places it for her to sit on)

Here you are. Ah, I almost forgot the wine. I got a Chablis. You like Chablis?

ANNE

Uh-huh.

(PAUL opens the bottle of wine and pours out two glasses. Meanwhile, ANNE is struggling to sit comfortably in the inflated chair with no success)

Well, that's remarkably uncomfortable, isn't it?

PAUL

(Takes chair from her)

There's a trick to it.

ANNE

I hope so.

PAUL

The salesman showed me. First you have to cross your legs.

(PAUL demonstrates how to sit in the chair and falls out of it in a backward somersault.)

(PAUL, disgusted, throws the chair out of the window into the courtyard. He then returns to the blanket and picks up the full wine glasses)

ANNE

You're quite a demented person, you know?

PAUL

Uh-huh.

(Hands her wine glass, she takes it)

To the loveliest leading baritone I know.

(They clink glasses and sip)

ANNE

Did you tell Janet where you were going?

PAUL

No. Did you tell Richard?

ANNE

No.

PAUL

Why not?

ANNE

I don't know. There wasn't time. He was calling long-distance from Cleveland on his way to a client dinner.

PAUL

How is old Richard?

ANNE

Old Richard is very well. He sold his design for a new supermarket.

PAUL

Old Richard is an architect.

ANNE

That's right.

                              PAUL

What does he design besides supermarkets?

                              ANNE

Mainly stores, but he has a commission to do a beach house.

                              PAUL

I'll watch the *Sunday Times Magazine* section.

                              ANNE

Do. One of the people he's meeting with asked him to design
a shopping complex. Not bad, huh?

                              PAUL

Very complex. Did he tell you all about it on the phone?

                              ANNE

Yes.

                              PAUL

Oh, I see. That's why you didn't have time to tell him.

                              ANNE

        (Coolly)

Your turn.

                              PAUL

Janet was making paella. Have you ever made it?

                              ANNE

No.

        (They look at each other)
    66

PAUL

Well, the trick in making a really superior paella is to get the chicken to brown and the clams to steam and the sausages to fry at the same time so they can be added to the rice at just the proper moment. Otherwise you get soggy rice. Then, too, overcooking can turn the golden yellow of saffron rice a warm beige which, although pleasing to look at is not a sign of really superior rice at our house.

(ANNE gives him a knowing look, which he sees)

She was not to be disturbed.

ANNE

A likely story.

PAUL

Every bit as likely as yours.

ANNE

(She has taken a chicken leg, now she stops eating it)

I think I'm feeling a little self-conscious. I just forgot how to swallow.

PAUL

(Has taken a bite of his sandwich)

Close your mouth and push.

(Beat)

I feel pretty self-conscious myself.

ANNE

Why didn't we tell them? It would have been so simple.

67

PAUL

Sure it would. "Hey, Janet, old liberated thing. I met this girl at the apartment you sent me to look at and we got to talking and she's a lot of laughs so I asked her out to dinner. Janet, stop crying in the paella. You're making it salty." Want a banana?

ANNE

No, thanks.

PAUL

How about an orange?

ANNE

Okay.

(He hands her one)

So we didn't tell them. Where's the harm?

PAUL

None at all. Of course, if they catch us it's headlines in the *West Side News*.

ANNE

Isn't this absurd?

PAUL

Absolutely.

ANNE

I feel so guilty.

PAUL

Me, too.

68

ANNE

(In a fake lawyer's voice)

And do you seriously expect the jury to believe, Mr. Friedman, that you and Mrs. Miller ate fruit salad and read comic books while on the floor of the aforementioned love nest?

PAUL

Objection! I move the last remark be stricken from the record, your honor.

ANNE

Objection sustained. While on the floor of this aforementioned apartment?

PAUL

I do, your honor. I further testify that at no time during our tryst . . .

ANNE

Objection.

PAUL

Assignation . . .

ANNE

Objection.

PAUL

Encounter?

(She makes no objection)

At no time during our encounter did Mrs. Miller ever lay a glove on me.

69

ANNE

Encounter. My God, we're having a brief encounter.

(With sudden seriousness)

Strike that from the record.

PAUL

(Picking up her mood)

You want to go, don't you?

ANNE

(Getting on her shoes)

Yes, I think so.

PAUL

You know how silly that is?

ANNE

Uh-huh.

PAUL

I mean, if Richard and Janet were here there'd be nothing wrong with it, would there?

ANNE

(Getting her coat)

Hardly.

PAUL

So? Nothing's happening they couldn't see. What's the problem?

70

ANNE

Paul, they're *not* here.

PAUL

(Gets up, runs to door and opens it)

Janet! Come on in! Plop yourself down. I'd like you to meet Anne. Anne, Janet.

(ANNE whirls around, then realizes he's playing)

She says she thinks you're awfully attractive.

ANNE

I think you're nuts.

PAUL

Janet?

ANNE

No, you.

PAUL

Oh. Haven't you forgotten something?

ANNE

What?

PAUL

You didn't introduce me to Richard.

ANNE

Oh, what the hell. Richard, this is my old friend, Paul Friedman. Paul and I were in *Show Boat* together. Richard says, "How are you, old man?"

71

PAUL

In the pink, buddy. In the pink. Had a little hernia trouble a while back, but everything's okay now.

ANNE

Richard says you looked like you might have had a little hernia trouble.

PAUL

Thanks, pal. Golly, Dick, you sure do sit up straight.

ANNE

Well, if it comes to that, what about Janet?

PAUL

Yeah, we're very proud of Janet's vertebrae at our house. Well, Janet has to go.

ANNE

I hope it's nothing Richard said.

PAUL

No, her group is sitting in at the George Washington Bridge until they build a Martha Washington Bridge. But she wants the three of us to stay and enjoy ourselves.

ANNE

That's very sweet.

PAUL

Aw, Richard has to go, too. He's designing poodle pissoirs for the East Side. Bye, Dick.

ANNE

(Sourly)

Nice meeting you, Janet.

PAUL

(Closes door)

Alone at last.

> (ANNE embarrassedly takes off her coat again and
> goes back to the blanket. She notices the yearbook
> again)

ANNE

Art and Literary Society, little theater . . .

PAUL

(Coming back to blanket)

Debating team and school paper.

ANNE

That doesn't seem like the background of a man who doesn't
want to do anything with his life.

PAUL

We're back to that, are we? Why are you so interested in my
lack of ambition?

ANNE

It seems a shame, that's all. When you were in college, wasn't
there something you wanted to do?

PAUL

I wanted to write sensitive, terribly perceptive short stories lay-

73

ing bare the vacuousness and hidden cruelties of the great Jewish middle class.

ANNE

What happened?

PAUL

Philip Roth.

ANNE

There must be room for one more sensitive Jewish author in the world.

PAUL

Yeah, I suppose they could squeeze me in, but I don't think I'm that sensitive any more.

ANNE

Nonsense.

PAUL

Look, will you leave the rest of my life to me, please?

(As they talk, the front door opens slowly and a middle-aged WOMAN peers in. She is the WOMAN in 4A)

ANNE

I'm sorry. As a very old friend I feel I have the right to pry.

WOMAN

What are you doing in here?

(They both jump up guiltily and unconsciously assume the positions that they were in when 4A questioned them through the hole in the door)

You heard me, what are you doing in here?

74

PAUL

It's all right. It's 4A. You remember us. We already passed inspection.

WOMAN

Oh, you. Damn, I knew there was something I was supposed to do.

(Calls over her shoulder into the hall)

Sit, Trixie! I see the doorknob's back.

PAUL

That's right.

WOMAN

You get the apartment?

PAUL

Yes, that's right. My wife and I have taken the apartment.

WOMAN

How much did you bribe?

PAUL	ANNE
Five Hundred.	Two thousand.
Two thousand.	Five hundred.

WOMAN

I suppose it's your own business. You'll be moving in soon. You have a dog?

PAUL	ANNE
No.	A schnauzer.

75

WOMAN

He's right, that's no dog. Couldn't protect you against a five-year-old.

ANNE

I don't usually need protection against five-year-olds. Except my own.

WOMAN

You haven't lived in this neighborhood. Well, as long as he doesn't shed I suppose it's all right. Trixie's allergic to dog hair.

(Looks at blanket covered with food)

Eating supper, huh?

PAUL

That's right. Would you care for a peach?

WOMAN

(Comes into room to blanket)

Don't mind. They cost an arm and a leg now. Sit, Trixie.

(She takes the peach PAUL gives her)

How much?

PAUL

Be my guest.

WOMAN

(Had no intention of paying)

No, how much did they soak you for them?

PAUL

Oh. Sixty-nine cents a pound.

WOMAN

(Looks "sucker" at him)

Are those grapes?

ANNE

(Becoming annoyed with her)

You mean the little round purple things? Are those grapes, Paul?

PAUL

(Picks up the grapes)

Would you care for some?

WOMAN

Don't mind.

PAUL

(Hands them to her)

Well, as long as you don't mind.

ANNE

How about an after dinner mint . . . Sit, Trixie!

WOMAN

No, but if you're not going to finish those bananas . . .

PAUL

(Picks them up)

Here you are. Bon appetit.

WOMAN

(Takes one of the discarded bags to carry the fruit)

Yeah, well, I'll leave you to do whatever it was you were going to do. I suppose I'll see you by the elevator sometime.

(As she exits)

Come on back in the house, Trixie. Back! Back! Back!

(PAUL closes the front door after her)

PAUL

Well, we got rid of her.

ANNE

What an awful woman.

PAUL

But well fed.

ANNE

I hope the fruit gives her gas. Why did you tell her we were married, Paul?

PAUL

I don't know, it seemed the simple thing to do.

ANNE

Because you were embarrassed.

PAUL

Here we go again. Analyzing our guilt.

ANNE

Tell me something honestly, would you?

PAUL

Sure.

78

ANNE

Do you have dinner with other women often?

PAUL

Other than who?

ANNE

I believe the name was Janet.

PAUL

Oh, her. Why do you want to know?

ANNE

I just do.

PAUL

Okay. No. I have never had dinner with another woman until tonight. I have never had an affair with another woman. I have never even flirted with another woman except twice . . . no . . . three times. Once at a New Year's party, once on the IRT and today.

ANNE

Are you flirting with me?

PAUL

Isn't it comfy here under the microscope?

ANNE

Are you?

PAUL

I think so. Don't you think so?

79

ANNE

I'm not sure.

PAUL

Boy, isn't my technique something? Nice and quiet. Now that we're playing the truth game, tell me something. Are you flirting back?

ANNE

No, of course not . . . I don't think so . . . I don't know . . . maybe.

PAUL

Can you check one of the above, please?

ANNE

I'm not sure I know what you mean by flirting. I mean I like you. You're very nice. But it does feel funny being here alone with you. I guess it feels exciting, sort of. Dangerous, maybe. A little bit wrong.

PAUL

Shall I call your analyst? You can describe it to him on the phone.

ANNE

How did you flirt with the girl on the IRT?

PAUL

Boy, you've got some set of ears there. All right, this sordid little tale began on the downtown platform at Eighty-sixth Street. It was morning. A misty, cool morning in late fall. The kind of a morning that makes a man recall his boyhood dreams of running away to sea or selling war bonds or writing sensitive short stories. There I was standing on the platform in my compromise bell bottoms when this girl walked by me. She wore an air of sensuality like other girls wear lipstick . . .

ANNE

Get to the climax.

PAUL

There was none. I was just flirting, remember? And stop skipping pages. She stopped at a gum machine to inspect her make-up . . .

ANNE

I thought she only wore an air of sensuality.

PAUL

See footnote. Footnote: She wore make-up in addition to an air of sensuality. Now shut up. Well, there she was looking at herself and there I was, looking at her, and suddenly our eyes met over the Dentyne machine. And in that moment, I panicked. I looked the other way. The number 1 train arrived

(He begins to pantomime the story)

and I squeezed past an old crippled lady and got a seat. I read one of the overhead ads about the heartbreak of psoriasis and how medical science has finally come up with a breakthrough which was available at local drugstores without a prescription, and I thought the AMA would have something to say about that. Then suddenly I saw a pair of knees. They seemed to have little smiling faces on them like a dog I once had that ran away and returned with fleas which we never did get rid of, so much for animal husbandry, but of course fleas aren't the scourge that psoriasis is. I looked higher. There were two thighs just about at my eye level. I can't tell you how disconcerting it is to see two thighs at your eye level before coffee. Suddenly all thoughts of Janet and our color TV which we watch from across the room because of radiation and our complete collection of

81

the operettas of Gilbert and Sullivan vanished from my mind. I looked higher.

(Reaction from ANNE)

Yes, gentle reader, I looked higher. There was a mini-skirt. Of red and blue and, yes, a touch of white. It was that same patriotic Dentyne-chewing nymphette standing before me, her thighs exposed for my personal pleasure, or so it seemed, her love beads dipping down over her pubescent breasts. She looked down at me and smiled. From beneath Max Factor's frosted moonglow number nine shone an array of teeth to light up the underground from Eighty-sixth to Borough Hall. Thirty-two Steinway keys in perfect tune.

ANNE

You saw all thirty-two? That must have been quite a smile.

PAUL

Don't interrupt. At that moment, I could have played concertos on those keys. I could have played a glissando to send Horowitz back into retirement. But I dared not.

ANNE

Chicken.

PAUL

Not so chicken I didn't smile back.

ANNE

We're up to sixty-four teeth.

PAUL

Sixty-three. I had a wisdom tooth extracted.

ANNE

Sorry about that.

PAUL

And then as if mesmerized, I stood up and did a crazy thing.

ANNE

What?

PAUL

I offered her my seat. And a gentleman of Latin persuasion took it. We stood there, smiling, hanging on juxtaposed straps and she spoke.

ANNE

Before you turn the page, more wine please.

PAUL

(Pours it for her)

You do manage to interrupt at the most awkward times.

ANNE

I know, but there's only so much perception a woman can take without a break. What'd she say?

PAUL

(Back in pantomime)

She said, "Some people."

ANNE

"Some people"?

PAUL

She was referring to the Latin gentleman.

ANNE

A biting remark.

83

PAUL

And so true. Well, one thing led to another, you know how it is . . .

ANNE

No, how is it?

PAUL

Friendly. And I found out my mini-seductress was a receptionist at a pajama manufacturing firm. She also played tennis, was a whiz at spaghetti and wanted to model.

ANNE

Your own Miss Subways.

PAUL

Then the train came into my station, I smiled, she smiled and I left.

ANNE

Is that all?

PAUL

Not quite. As the doors closed, from my position of safety on the platform, I winked at her.

ANNE

And what did she do?

PAUL

She winked back. And that is what is known in the trade as a Jewish affair.

ANNE

So, you've never flirted with another woman.

PAUL

I see the symbolism of my story went completely over your head. I had stripped that girl naked on the downtown number 1 train and ravaged her without missing my stop.

ANNE

You're very sweet.

PAUL

Thank you, I am.

(Sits on the blanket next to her)

Now, what about you? Anything torrid you'd care to contribute?

ANNE

Nothing as sensational. Only once an editor got me behind the filing cabinets and asked me up to his apartment.

PAUL

Yeah?

ANNE

That's all.

PAUL

Did you call Richard at the office hysterical?

ANNE

I held off till supper.

PAUL

And what did he say?

ANNE

He said the steak was tough.

PAUL

Yeah. There's America out there screwing each other like bunnies and here we are, two old faithfuls, without a spurt of water between us.

ANNE

You want water?

PAUL

No.

ANNE

I do.

(Rising with her glass and exits into the dining room)

PAUL

(Calling after her)

You know what we are? Extinct. Our whole generation went by like a damp sparkler. Oh, we had a few things going for us for a while. The cha-cha, white bucks, D.A.'s, D.J.'s, J.D.'s, Your Show of Shows . . .

(Sings)

So long for a while
That's all the songs for a while
So long to Your Hit Parade

And the tunes that you picked to be played
So long*

    (Beat)

But by and large we just held the door for the kids today. I wonder if any of them know what it's like to be faithful. Hey, do you realize we're the only generation that wondered whether or nor Franny was pregnant?

                    ANNE

    (Off-stage)

Paul!

                    PAUL

Where are you today, Holden Caulfield?

                    ANNE

    (Rushes back in with faucet fixture in her hand)

Paul, the faucet broke off in my hand.

                    PAUL

Keep it.

                    ANNE

I can't get it back on and the water's pouring out.

                    PAUL

Let it pour.

                    ANNE

But the sink's stopped up. Paul, it's going to flood. Let's get out of here.

* Lyrics from "So Long for a While" words and music by Irving Chansky. Reprinted by permission of American Tobacco Company.

(He goes with her through dining room into kitchen, makes an off-stage exclamation, then they return)

PAUL

Sorry, there's no time to build an ark. I'll get the super.

(Takes faucet from her)

Why does it always rain on picnics?

ANNE

Hurry, it's really pouring out.

PAUL

Okay, there's a room between us and the tidal wave, relax.

(Singing as he leaves)

It's the Toast of the Town
The pride and boast of the town
The absolute top . . ."

(He makes false exit into closet)

*. . . the cream of the crop. . .**

(He exits.

Anne watches him go, smiling. She thinks for a moment, then)

ANNE

(Sings)

Cream of Wheat
it's so good to eat
yes, we have it every day.

* Lyrics from theme song of "Toast of the Town" by Ray Bloch, Minna Brown Lewis and Robert Arthur. Copyright 1954 by Anne-Rachel Music Corporation. Used by permission.

*We sing this song
cause it makes us strong
and it makes us shout hurray!* Hooray!*

(She picks up one of the comic books)

Wonder Woman.

(Reads)

"Great Aphrodite, Steve! Without my wrist and ankle bracelets
I am as weak as any mortal woman!" Poor thing.

PAUL

(Entering)

I told the elevator man. I didn't know whether or not you could
tread water.

(ANNE throws down the comic book, PAUL notices)

Isn't it terrific?

ANNE

Terrific. Let's go.

PAUL

Why?

ANNE

The super will be here in a minute.

PAUL

So what? I'll tell him we took the apartment. Relax, will you?
Sit down and have some more wine. If you'd stuck to the wine,
this whole thing never would have happened.

* Lyrics from commercial for "Cream of Wheat" a trademark of Nabisco,
Inc. Reprinted by permission of Telegeneral Corporation.

ANNE

This whole thing is crazy.

PAUL

(Picking up comic book)

Don't you love the art work? Did you notice how Wonder Woman's breasts are always so well defined?

ANNE

I can't say I did.

PAUL

Well, they are. I had a dream about her. We were alone on a distant planet and she let me look under her ankle bracelets.

ANNE

You were a hot little kid.

PAUL

What kid? I had the dream a couple of months ago.
(ANNE takes the comic book from him and hits him on the head with it, then throws it down)

ANNE

Look, I have a compromise.
(She gets up and puts on her coat)
We've eaten. Let's take a stroll.

PAUL

Why? It can't be that you're afraid of the super. You afraid of me?

ANNE

Of course not.

PAUL

Never mind "of course not." I'll bet you are.

ANNE

What would I have to be afraid of?

PAUL

That I'd try something funny.

ANNE

Don't be silly.

PAUL

Well, you don't have to worry. I thought about it on line at the A&P but I decided not to.

ANNE

Why?

PAUL

Not because I don't think you're "that kind" of girl. I'm not that much of a fifties person. I just thought it would be dishonest.

ANNE

How?

PAUL

Because I got you here in a different way.

91

ANNE

And besides, we're the faithful type, remember?

PAUL

Yup. Not that it would hurt either of us to have a little fling. Hell, it'd probably do us some good. Besides, I've always wanted to know what it's like, haven't you?

ANNE

Well, it's only natural for me to wonder what it would be like to have a man other than Richard make love to me.

PAUL

He was your first?

ANNE

My one and only.
(Winces. Turns away from him)
I didn't mean to let that out.

PAUL

Why not?

ANNE

It sounds so old maidish.

PAUL

At the risk of sounding slightly Edwardian, I respect you for it.

ANNE

Do you really? Think before answering, please.

PAUL

(Pause)

I don't know.

ANNE

See? Even among the virtuous, virtue has had it. You don't know
how lucky you were, being a boy. You could experiment without a qualm.

PAUL

Now you sound like Janet.

ANNE

Don't knock her, she's right. Us "good girls" will always wonder, does every man hold a woman the same way? Do they all
make funny little noises? Are some of them stronger or gentler
or . . .

(Paul has started to caress her)

What are you doing, Paul?

PAUL

(Takes his hand away)

I was about to try something funny.

ANNE

Remember the A&P.

PAUL

I'm sorry.

ANNE

I suppose I'm the type that will always wonder and never do

anything about it. What was it like, making love to different girls?

PAUL

I don't think I'm the right guy to ask.

ANNE

Why? Were you a virgin, too?

PAUL

No! God forbid. Boys weren't allowed to be virgins. They wouldn't let you on the track team if you were . . . No, I was very experienced. There was the professional lady my cousin took me to who watched TV with the sound off. And there was the girl who washed dishes in the school cafeteria. I later found out she was retarded. And . . . there was the mistress of the little theater group. But the only reason she let me, and believe me, she let me, she didn't join me, was that she thought someday I'd be a star. So you see, in my own way I was a virgin too, when I met Janet.

ANNE

Can I tell you something without your moving closer?

PAUL

Try me.

ANNE

I think Janet's a lucky girl.

PAUL

Thank you. Can I tell you something?

ANNE

Go ahead.

(The front door opens and EDDIE enters carrying his tool box)

EDDIE

You got a flood?

PAUL

In the kitchen.

(Gives him broken fixture)

Here's the faucet.

(Nervously)

Oh, if you're wondering what we're doing here, my wife and I have taken the apartment and we wanted to have our first meal here without the kids bothering us.

EDDIE

I wasn't wondering.

(A look at the blanket)

Peaches, huh?

PAUL

Yeah. Here you are.

(Hands him one. EDDIE takes the peach and exits into the dining room)

Still nervous?

ANNE

Still telling people we're married?

PAUL

Still feeling guilty?

95

ANNE

What did you want to tell me?

PAUL

Just this . . .

(The WOMAN from 4A comes in)

WOMAN

Did I hear Eddie come in here?

PAUL

In the kitchen.

WOMAN

(Over her shoulder into the hall)

Sit, Trixie!

(As she crosses to dining room)

For thirty-nine cents, the peach was delicious. For sixty-nine, it was mealy.

(Exits)

ANNE

Go on.

PAUL

Can we wait till the train pulls out?

ANNE

No, tell me while there are people around to protect me.

PAUL

All right. I think if I ever did want to have an affair, I'd want
to have it with you.

ANNE

Thank you.

PAUL

(Quickly)

And I want to have an affair.

ANNE

(Rises)

Paul . . .

PAUL

(Follows her)

I can't help it. I'm thirty-three going on fifty and I have no
hobbies and even though I'm making jokes, I'm dead serious.
I feel a little lost and I think you do, too.

ANNE

You don't find your way when you're lost by going to someone
else's house.

PAUL

I'm not so sure.

(EDDIE and the WOMAN enter)

WOMAN

Eddie, my sink's been leaking since Eisenhower was President.
Theirs just started.

97

EDDIE

Theirs was flooding. When yours is flooding, I'll fix it.

WOMAN

Eddie, Christmas is coming.

EDDIE

You don't tip at Christmas.

WOMAN

Maybe I'll mend my ways this Christmas.

EDDIE

Maybe I'll fix the faucet New Year's.

WOMAN

Eddie, I'm an old lady! All alone in the world!

EDDIE

(He cannot get out the door because of the presence of Trixie)

You got that killer to keep you company.

WOMAN

My little Trixie a killer? Sit, Trixie!

EDDIE

(To PAUL)

The last guy who went into her apartment had to lock himself in the stall shower.

WOMAN

Eddie, you want to get out of here?

EDDIE

Si.

WOMAN

Trixie's in the hall.

EDDIE

I'll fix your faucet.

WOMAN

I'll restrain her.

(As she exits)

Sit, Trixie! See? A big dog comes in handy sometimes.

EDDIE

(As he exits)

Caramba, que vieja esta! Me tiene fastidiad con el carajo perro ese. Se lo voy a envenenar.

(Caramba, this old lady! She's got me screwed up with that damn dog. I'm going to poison it.)

(They are gone. ANNE and PAUL remain quiet for a moment. There is a tenseness between them)

PAUL

Where were we?

ANNE

Sara Lee, please.

PAUL

Chocolate swirl okay?

99

ANNE

Fine.

PAUL

I take it the subject is dropped.

ANNE

Right.

PAUL

(Opens the tin of Sara Lee, peels back the protective
film and hands the whole thing to her)

What a technique I have. How many guys do you know try
to seduce a girl by asking permission?

ANNE

(Cuts into cake, but never really eats any)

Not many.

PAUL

At least you've got to admit, I'm not hard sell.

ANNE

I don't want to talk about it, please.

PAUL

That's the trouble. We talked too much. We talked ourselves
out of it.

ANNE

We were never in it.

PAUL

I suppose not. Pity.

ANNE

And if we were, where would that have left Janet?

PAUL

Where she's always been.

ANNE

At home with the kids and linoleum.

PAUL

It's not like that. There are lots of things married people can't share.

ANNE

Like affairs?

PAUL

(Beat)

It wouldn't have hurt Janet because she never would have known about it. It would have been just for me. Something to prove that I'm well, still a *man*—somebody a woman might find attractive. I'm sorry, but I still want to have an affair with you.

ANNE

I wish you'd stop saying that. It sounds so. . .

PAUL

I know, like Andy Hardy trying to make out.

ANNE

No . . . yes. Look, I'm no one to talk. I'm the one they patterned Doris Day after.

(Starts to move away)

I'm going. I really am. I know there are a hundred psychologically sound sociologically uplifting reasons why we should have an affair, but . . .

(She crosses to door, then stops)

Goodbye, Paul.

(Beat)

I hope you have your affair someday. If it means that much to you, I hope you meet someone you can have it with.

PAUL

(He has made no move to stop her and now does not look at her)

Sure.

ANNE

It won't take long. You've decided now.

PAUL

Is that the way you see it? I've decided to have an affair so I'll just sniff around till I have one? You forget. I'm a virgin, too. You were special, Anne. You're a very special person.

ANNE

(Pause)

You're pretty special yourself. But I love Richard.

PAUL

And I love Janet. I do. Truly.

ANNE

I know you do.

PAUL

But what I need I can't get from Janet just because she *is* my wife. Isn't the same true for you?

ANNE

I suppose. But . . .

PAUL

But what?

ANNE

But I was raised in the forties. I was taught a lot of things about what a nice woman is. Maybe some of them were wrong, but I learned them.

PAUL

You could unlearn them.

ANNE

I don't think so.
  (Pause)

For what it's worth, Paul. I would like to go to bed with you.

PAUL
  (Averting his gaze)

I'll bet you say that to all the boys.

ANNE

I mean it. And nobody is more surprised than I am.

PAUL

Then I think you're making a mistake.

ANNE

Could be. Goodbye.

(ANNE turns to go out the door. She has her hand on the doorknob, but does not move. Her back is to PAUL and the audience. PAUL senses her change. There is a long pause as he collects himself)

PAUL

Anne. Turn out the lights.

(ANNE turns out the lights, then turns into the room, taking off her coat very slowly, and leaves it on the railing. PAUL rises to his knees in place looking at her, remembers the cassette and turns it on. It begins to play Chopin's Minute Waltz. PAUL rises)

The Minute Waltz?

(Outside the window, it begins to rain. ANNE comes to PAUL, after a moment they begin to embrace)

CURTAIN

END OF ACT ONE

ACT TWO

SCENE 1

The apartment, the next morning. There is no evidence of the activities of the previous night except for an orange peel in the middle of the floor.

The front door opens and JANET enters, followed by PAUL. She is quite attractive, well-dressed. He seems depressed.

PAUL

Janet, I don't see why we had to come here. I told you I didn't like it.

JANET

Honey, it's rent-controlled. Besides, you always liked Ruthie's upstairs. It's the same apartment.

(Looks around)

Oh, look at it!

PAUL

You look at it.

JANET

Paul, what's with you? Does your stomach hurt?

PAUL

Why?

JANET

Because you sound like your stomach hurts. And you ate cold paella for breakfast.

PAUL

I feel fine.

JANET

I should have picked out the clams.

PAUL

I like cold clams. They wake you up.

JANET

Are you mad because of last night?

PAUL

What about last night?

JANET

What do you mean, what about last night? I had the girls over. I mean, the women. Are you getting threatened?

PAUL

No, I'm not getting threatened.

JANET

You're threatened.

PAUL

I'm not threatened!

JANET

Then what was that performance about when you came home?

PAUL

What performance?

JANET

What performance? Who emptied the ashtrays, made the coffee
and served cookies?

PAUL

I was trying to be helpful.

JANET

Uh-huh. May I see the kitchen now?
      (She exits into dining room)

PAUL

I want a club chair!

JANET

      (Returns)

What?

PAUL

I want a club chair.

JANET

Now?

PAUL

I've always wanted a club chair.

JANET

Okay.

PAUL

Well, you're my wife! You ought to know these things!

JANET

All right, now I know. Is there anything else you want me to know?

PAUL

A man has a right to sprawl out if he wants to.

JANET

Be my guest. Meanwhile, I'm going to check out the kitchen.

(JANET goes into the dining room. PAUL sees the orange peel on the floor, dives for it, hides it, then realizes his foolishness and drops it back on the floor)

PAUL

I don't like it!

JANET

(Re-enters)

For crying out loud, why not?

PAUL

Because it's . . . uh . . . uh . . .

JANET

Paul, please, please like this six room, rent-controlled apartment for three twenty-five. I'll do anything you like! I'll call your mother "mom."

PAUL

All right. All right.

JANET

I'm going to see the kitchen.

PAUL

Janet, if you go into that kitchen, I won't be here when you come out!

JANET

And just where will you be?

PAUL

(Groping for an answer, finding none and deflating)

Home.

JANET

(Going to him)

Sweetheart, whatever is going on, please—please don't let it stop us from getting this apartment. We need it. There's a maid's room out there that could be your workroom. You could write there like you used to.

PAUL

(Beat)

I love you.

JANET

I love you, too. Now may I see the kitchen?

PAUL

I really do want a club chair.

JANET

I'll meet you for lunch Monday and we'll get you one.

PAUL

What's a Morris chair?

JANET

I don't know. Are you getting a fetish? Maybe I have a Gelusil in my bag. Next time, I'll freeze the leftovers.

> (They exit into the dining room. In a moment, the front door opens and RICHARD enters. He wears a business suit and carries an attache case. He's good-looking)

RICHARD

> (Calling out the door)

Come on, honey. It's not a dentist's office.

> (Pause)

Annie, it's rent-controlled!

ANNE

> (Enters wearing dark glasses, her coat collar up, her hat brim down. She does not want to come into the room)

Okay, look.

RICHARD

Hey, this is nice! I knew it couldn't be as bad as you painted it. It's big! Of course, you're right, the moldings have to go.

> (He looks out window)

And it needs some kind of window treatment so we don't see the bricks eroding.

112

(He has put his attache case standing on the floor between the front door and the bedroom hall, now sits on the radiator cover)

But there's a lot of potential here.

ANNE

I hate it.

RICHARD

You don't hate it.

ANNE

I hate it.

RICHARD

You couldn't hate it.

ANNE

I can and do.

RICHARD

You don't. You just think you do.

ANNE

(Turns)

Could we go now?

RICHARD

Annie, six rooms . . .

BOTH

. . . for three and a quarter . . .

113

ANNE

I'll wait outside.

RICHARD

(Goes to her)

You're in a lousy mood this morning, aren't you? What's the matter? Did you miss me?

(Embraces her)

ANNE

Richard . . .

RICHARD

Come on, I'm home now. You know what?

(His attention back to the room)

I could put a second level in front of the windows.

ANNE

A what?

RICHARD

A platform. You know, like that bank I did in Greenwich, remember?

ANNE

Oh . . . that step *up* everybody kept tripping over?

RICHARD

Nobody tripped over my platform.

ANNE

I did.

114

RICHARD

Then learn to lift your feet like everybody else.

ANNE

I'm sorry, I was too tall for ballet.

RICHARD

(Mutters)

Oh, Christ.

(Continues planning room)

With ceilings this high, I can hang furniture.

ANNE

Why not.

RICHARD

Remember that great idea I had for a hanging conversation pit?
It could work right here.

ANNE

I can hardly wait.

RICHARD

Annie . . .

ANNE

(Suddenly, with more emotion than is called for)

I don't want to live in a Bloomingdale's room, Richard! I'm not
that good a person!

RICHARD

You want an aspirin?

115

ANNE

(With weary sadness, as if she's said it many times)

I want a regular lower-class home like everybody else. I want
direct lighting. God, how I want direct lighting! And petunias
in window boxes, not jungle plants! Richard, I want to be
downward mobile!

RICHARD

(Said lightly as if he's heard it many times)

You're getting hysterical.

ANNE

Why not? I'm too goddam calm all the time.

RICHARD

(Turns away, then back)

All right, you want to tell me what I did now?

ANNE

You didn't do anything.

RICHARD

My mother called last night, right?

ANNE

Your mother didn't do anything.

RICHARD

Your mother? Alexa? Nicky?

ANNE

Nobody did anything. Richard, you're too good for me.

116

RICHARD

Yeah, it looks that way, doesn't it.

(Coaxes her off platform)

Come on, Annie, let's go look at the kitchen.

(They walk to the dining room doors. JANET and PAUL enter at the same time. ANNE and PAUL stare at each other in horror. Neither RICHARD nor JANET pays any attention to their mates or each other. The two couples exit, JANET and PAUL into the bedrooms. Beat. PAUL's head appears from the bedrooms, ANNE's from dining room. They motion wildly to each other. They disappear. Beat. ANNE and PAUL rush back)

ANNE

(In an embarrassed whisper, terribly awkward)

Hello.

PAUL

Hello. Is that Richard?

ANNE

Uh-huh. Janet?

PAUL

Yeah. I told her I had to go to the bathroom.

ANNE

I'm supposed to be measuring the room.

(Does some awkward pacing)

PAUL

What happened to you last night?

ANNE

I went home.

PAUL

Why didn't you wake me up?

ANNE

You looked so comfortable, lying there, cuddling the chicken.
(Off-stage a loud banging is heard as RICHARD tests the walls, they break apart at the sound, then come back together when no one enters)

PAUL

You should have woken me.

ANNE

I had to get home to pay the baby sitter.
(He leads her further Downstage away from the dining room door)

PAUL

Are you all right?

ANNE

As well as can be expected. And you?

PAUL

Okay. When did Richard get home?

ANNE

This morning. How was Janet's meeting?

PAUL

Fine. They're going to blow something up.

ANNE

That's nice.

> (Sees orange peel, runs for it and puts it in her coat pocket)

Oh, my God!

> (She makes sounds as if appreciating the room to cover her outburst)

PAUL

It's only an orange peel. It doesn't have our names on it.

ANNE

You look tired.

PAUL

I was up half the night.

ANNE

Who wasn't?

PAUL

I was writing a story.

ANNE

Really?

PAUL

Yes.

ANNE

I'm glad.

PAUL

I'd like to talk to you.

ANNE

I'd better get back.

PAUL

(After a beat, extends his hand, she takes it)

All right. Goodbye, Anne.

ANNE

Goodbye, Paul.

(At that moment, JANET enters from the bedroom. They race apart, PAUL to the closet door, ANNE to her pacing)

ANNE

Hi!

JANET

Hi.

(ANNE exits into dining room)

PAUL

(Covering for his frozen position)

This closet's no good.

JANET

Really?

(She enters it and is lost inside. As she returns)

What are you talking about? It's huge.

PAUL

That's just it. It's a whole lot of wasted space.

JANET

I hope Ruthie has Maalox.

ANNE

(ANNE leads RICHARD out of the dining room)

Okay, let's go.

PAUL

(To JANET)

Come on, let's go.

RICHARD

I haven't seen the bedrooms.

JANET

I want to check the refrigerator again.

(As RICHARD and JANET, with their spouses trying to hide, pass each other, they stop with signs of recognition)

RICHARD

Janet?

JANET

Richie? Oh, for heaven's sake!

(ANNE and PAUL appear to be dying of shock and terror)

RICHARD

For crying out loud. What has it been, a century?

JANET

Just about.

RICHARD

Well, you certainly don't look a century older.

JANET

I don't believe it . . . Richard, come meet my husband, Paul Friedman. Paul, meet Richard . . . I'm sorry.

RICHARD

Miller.

JANET

Of course. An old neighbor and the best hide and seek player on the block.

(RICHARD extends his hand and gets a limp fish hand-shake from PAUL)

PAUL

How do.

RICHARD

And this is my wife, Anne. Anne, Janet *Gordon!*

(He is happy he remembered)

PAUL

Very good. But it's Friedman now.

RICHARD

That's right.

ANNE

(Numb)

Just like her husband's. Fancy that. Hello.

(RICHARD helps ANNE to shake JANET's hand)

RICHARD

Janet and I grew up on the same block.

ANNE

Wow.

PAUL

It's been nice. Let's go.

JANET

Paul! Forgive him, he ate clams this morning.

PAUL

They wake you up.

RICHARD

Are you looking at the apartment, too?

JANET

Yes. It's lovely, isn't it?

RICHARD

Very nice. I hope we don't end up competing for it. That'd
be a hell of a way to get reacquainted.

(ANNE starts to laugh, her face a mixture of fear and
numbness)

123

ANNE

Anybody for a quick game of hide and seek?

RICHARD

What's so funny?

ANNE

Funny? Nothing. Is somebody laughing?

RICHARD

Yes, dear. You are.

ANNE

Oh, I'll stop.

(But her laughter is hysterical and she can't stop)

RICHARD

What did *you* eat this morning?

(Despite himself, PAUL has started to laugh, too)

JANET

What are you laughing at?

PAUL

Me? I don't know.

ANNE

Look, I think I'll go hide my eyes in the kitchen. Anyone around my base is it. Nice meeting you.

(She exits into dining room, laughing)

JANET

(Embarrassed)

Well, Richard, you're looking marvelous. Tell me about yourself. What do you do?

RICHARD

I'm an architect.

(Off-stage, ANNE laughs. He reacts, then continues)

What about you? Any kids?

JANET

(Looks at PAUL, he is in another world)

A boy, Joshua.

RICHARD

We've got two. Aleva and . . .

(He fumbles due to tension)

. . . and Nicky. I think they must have given their mother a hard time this morning.

JANET

Oh, well . . .

RICHARD

She's really quite sane, most of the time.

JANET

Then she's ahead of the game.

(Off-stage burst of laughter)

We've really got to go. It was wonderful seeing you again, Richard.

(JANET and RICHARD embrace in parting. At that moment ANNE enters, in control. She sees the embrace and starts to laugh again, exiting immediately)

RICHARD

(Looking after her, bewildered)

I apologize for the maniac.

JANET

No need to. I hope we run into each other again.

RICHARD

Just follow the sound of laughter. Good seeing you, Janet. Nice meeting you, Saul.

PAUL

Paul.

RICHARD

I'd better go get Minniehaha. I've got to leave, too.

(He exits into dining room)

JANET

Let's go upstairs to Ruthie's.

PAUL

I think I'll take another look around. Maybe I'll change my mind.

JANET

Good.

(Fondly to PAUL)

Poor Richard.

(JANET exits. RICHARD and ANNE enter)

RICHARD

Now, what the hell was that all about? Oh, hi, Saul.

PAUL

Hi.

(He paces his way into the bedrooms, knocking RICHARD's attache case on the way. RICHARD reacts)

ANNE

I just got the giggles, that's all.

RICHARD

Over what?

ANNE

Nothing. Sorry.

RICHARD

What's the matter with you today? Are you pregnant?!

ANNE

No.

(Beat. With emphasis)

No! Just let it pass. Okay, Richard?

RICHARD

I introduce you to someone and you get hysterical.

ANNE

(Looking for some excuse to appease him)

It was the hanging conversation pit. I kept picturing the four of us, hanging and talking over old times, and swaying.

RICHARD

That's funny.

127

(Gets his attache case)

I've got to get to the office. You coming?

ANNE

No, I think I'll take another look around.

RICHARD

Try to like it, huh? And get to the agent? Are you in control now?

ANNE

Yes. So much in control I'm getting morose.

RICHARD

I'll see you this evening.

ANNE

Goodbye, dear.

(RICHARD exits, imitating PAUL's pacing. She stands there a moment. PAUL enters from the bedrooms, still pacing)

PAUL

Hello again.

ANNE

Hello. Where's Janet?

PAUL

Upstairs with a friend.

(ANNE checks the outside hall to see if RICHARD is gone, closes the door and sighs with relief)

I'm sorry that had to happen.

128

ANNE

Me, too. You wouldn't happen to have some Harvey's Bristol Cream Sherry on you, would you?

PAUL

Sorry. Settle for some Trident Sugarless Chewing Gum?
(Produces some from pocket)

ANNE

What the hell. No, thanks.

PAUL

Richard seems very nice.

ANNE

Yes, he is. Janet seems very nice.

PAUL

Yeah.
(There is an awkward silence as gloom descends)

ANNE

Well . . .

PAUL

Can I say something?

ANNE

Paul, I think it would be better if you didn't, okay?

PAUL

Okay.

129

ANNE

(Beat)

Goodbye, Paul.

PAUL

Goodbye, Anne.

(They stand there, waiting for each other to leave)

ANNE

Isn't one of us going somewhere?

PAUL

Sure.

(PAUL goes to the front door and tries to open it. The doorknob comes off in his hand. ANNE does not see this happen. He tries to replace it and the sound of the doorknob on the outside of the door falling is heard. PAUL stretches out his hand with the doorknob to ANNE without looking, but she is not looking either and doesn't see. He starts to laugh)

ANNE

Please go, Paul.

(He has his back to her, heaving with laughter)

Please?

(She turns and sees him)

Don't cry, Paul. Please don't cry.

(He holds the doorknob out to her again. She sees it, utters a cry and sits on the radiator cover, burying her head in her arms. She is making indeterminate sounds—either laughing or crying)

130

PAUL

Are you laughing or crying?

ANNE

I don't know.

PAUL

(Dropping the doorknob)

Do you know yet?

ANNE

(Sitting up)

My teeth are showing, so I must be laughing. Please get us out of here.

PAUL

Is it so awful being here with me?

ANNE

It's not my idea of fun.

PAUL

(Calls through the peephole)

Hello? 4A? It's 4B again!
(Turns back)

Why is it so awful?

ANNE

I don't know. It just is. Please.

PAUL

I'm sorry.

(Calling out again)

Hello? Hello?

(He listens)

Nothing.

ANNE

Why don't I just jump?

PAUL

And I thought guilt was exclusively a Jewish phenomenon.

ANNE

If you wanted to find someone as guilty as me, you'd have to go all the way to Argentina.

PAUL

Not quite. You'd just have to cross the room.

ANNE

(With a small, kind smile)

We certainly are a sophisticated pair, aren't we?

PAUL

Nope.

ANNE

Well, what do we do now?

PAUL

We talk.

ANNE

To coin a phrase, there really is nothing to talk about.

PAUL

I don't agree. We did something important last night. I think
we ought to discuss it.

ANNE

All right. What do you want to say? Something witty? Go
ahead, make me laugh. Say, don't you ever work?

PAUL

I'm on vacation this week.

ANNE

You going to write a report on what you did on your vacation?

(She moves away from him to down right)

PAUL

You're really out to get yourself, aren't you? You don't deserve
it.

ANNE

You mean that was somebody else here last night. What a relief! Now I can get back to my linoleum with a clear con-
science.

PAUL

We do what we have to do.

ANNE

Look, it's very sweet of you to want to ease my mind, but I
really think it would be best if I just went home and did a little
private penance. Don't worry, it's no big deal. I'll make Richard
a rib roast or something. What the hell, it's the least I can do.

PAUL

And what do I do?

133

ANNE

Buy her a present.

PAUL

It won't help.

ANNE

(Kindly)

Don't be a sap. Men are allowed their little flings. Everybody knows that.

PAUL

That's not what I mean. What do I do about you?

ANNE

Nothing.

PAUL

I don't want to do nothing.

ANNE

Paul . . .

PAUL

I want to see you again.

ANNE

You're crazy.

PAUL

I know. This whole thing is crazy. It's completely out of context with the rest of my life. I don't even read *Playboy*. Tomorrow night?

134

ANNE

Stop it.

PAUL

The night after? Or the night after that?

ANNE

If you don't stop, Paul, I'll lock myself in the bathroom.

PAUL

Okay, just don't touch the doorknob.
    (Beat)
All right. I'm sorry.
        (There is a pause while both stand still not knowing
        where to go from there)

ANNE

So—what's your story about?

PAUL

The girl on the IRT. It's not much of a story, though.

ANNE

Why?

PAUL

Nothing happens. She pulls away and he lets her.

ANNE

    (With resignation, sadly)
What else could he do?

135

PAUL

He could have stayed on the train with her.

ANNE

No, he couldn't do that.

PAUL

Why not? Millions of people do.

ANNE

But not him. He's married and has a child. And she's married and has children. And that's that.

PAUL

The girl on the IRT wasn't married, but let it pass.

ANNE

There's no future in it, Paul. All it can get us is pain.

PAUL

Not as much pain as never seeing you again.

ANNE

Look, let's open the window and yell. Somebody's bound to hear us.

PAUL

I take it the subject is dropped.

ANNE

Right.

PAUL

One-two-three help?

(PAUL opens the window and they solemnly take their places in front of it)

ANNE

Fine.

PAUL

One-two-three . . .

BOTH

HELP!

PAUL

One-two-three . . .

BOTH

HELP!

PAUL

One-two-three . . .

BOTH

HELP!

(He suddenly kisses her. She stands there in his arms, rigid, neither fighting nor giving in to the kiss. Then her body relaxes and she throws her arms around him)

PAUL

We take long lunch hours in advertising. Two hours.

ANNE

I have two children to feed lunch.

137

PAUL

You could get a woman in.

ANNE

You can't get a woman for two hours a day.

PAUL

You can if you want to.

ANNE

(Breaking away)

No!

PAUL

(Seeing that her mind is set again; beat)

One-two-three . . .

BOTH

HELP!

PAUL

One-two-three . . .

BOTH

HELP!

PAUL

There are agencies for part-time help.

ANNE

My neighbor's girl is in college. She might . . .

(Suddenly ANNE has given in to him. They embrace, this time passionately. And just as suddenly, she pushes away from him and runs to the front door. She looks out the peephole and remains that way as if she will not move until someone comes to rescue them. PAUL watches her, a feeling of resignation slowly coming over him. Realizing the agony she's in, he looks for a way to help. He sees a ledge outside the window that leads to another apartment. He decides to try it. He takes off his jacket, straightens himself up with bravado and steps out of the window and along the ledge until he's out of view. ANNE has seen none of this. She turns back into the room)

ANNE

Paul, I . . . Paul?

(She looks off to the dining room and assumes he's there)

We can't see each other any more, Paul. You must understand that. No matter how much we want to. We're not the kind of people to enter into anything lightly and we're also not the kind of people to hurt those we love, so what can it possibly come to? I have enough pain in my life, Paul. I don't want any more.

(He comes back in view on the ledge, moaning with fright. She assumes he's crying and goes, she thinks to him in the dining room)

Paul?

(She returns to the living room still hearing him, puzzled. Then she sees him)

Paul!

(Her shout startles him and he loses his footing. She runs to help him)

Paul!

(She catches him and helps him inside. They sit on the radiator cover)

What were you doing out there?

PAUL

I thought I could crawl to the next apartment.

ANNE

(Kissing him)

You idiot! We're four flights up!

PAUL

I didn't want to hurt you any more.

ANNE

(Now all her arguments and fears disappear. He has risked his life for her)

You idiot. How am I ever gonna get rid of you?

(They hold each other for a moment)

PAUL

Now what do we do?

ANNE

(Troubled, but resigned to it)

I guess we have an affair.

PAUL

Do you mean it?

ANNE

What else can I do? You're willing to kill yourself for me. How big an ingrate do you think I am?

(This last with a faint smile)

PAUL

Come with me now.

ANNE

(Looks at door with missing knob)

How? Besides, the kids are with a sitter. And my cleaning woman's in today. If I don't watch her she doesn't wax. She buffs.

PAUL

Tonight?

ANNE

The Myerses are coming over. He's an undertaker.

PAUL

You don't know an undertaker.

ANNE

I do.

PAUL

I know a tree surgeon.

ANNE

Good.

141

PAUL

My God, does he tell you about his work?

ANNE

Uh-huh. It's fascinating. Do you know where they put the tube for the formaldehyde?

PAUL

Friday night?

ANNE

(Beat. Finally a smile)

Friday night.

PAUL

And this time I'll take you out to dinner. To the fanciest restaurant in town. The Grenouille.

ANNE

The Grenouille? Is that the kind of place people have affairs in?

PAUL

You don't have it there. You just eat there.

ANNE

We can't. The Grenerts go there for their anniversary every year and I don't remember when it is.

PAUL

Ask them.

ANNE

And some times the Geyers go there to make up after a fight.

PAUL

Call and make sure they're getting along.

ANNE

Someplace a little more discreet, please.

    (Beat)

How did Bette Davis and Paul Henreid always manage it?

PAUL

Room service. I'll order up from room service. The Plaza? The Waldorf? The St. Regis?

ANNE

Too expensive.

PAUL

How about the Hotel Albert on University Place? It's clean and reasonable.

ANNE

Suits me.

    (She rises and moves away. Suddenly she smiles, he
    notices)

PAUL

What?

ANNE

I'm wondering what I should wear. Gloria Grahame had a terrific outfit for adultery in *The Bad and the Beautiful*. Should I bring a nightgown?

PAUL

Suit yourself.

ANNE

Are you going to bring pajamas?

PAUL

I wasn't planning on sleeping.

ANNE

I think I'll wear something inconspicuous. Like a paper bag over my head.

PAUL

Don't chicken out on me.

ANNE

I won't.

(Almost in tears)

And nobody'll know. And nobody'll get hurt, right?

PAUL

That's right.

ANNE

Promise me that. Promise me nobody'll know and nobody'll get hurt.

PAUL

I promise.

ANNE

(Pulls herself together and puts on a brave smile)

So, what should we have room service send us?

PAUL

Hey, I just remembered. There's a wonderful little restaurant around the corner from the hotel where they make the best veal piccata . . .

ANNE

Next to the sandal shop?

PAUL

Right!

ANNE

Don't have the piccata.

PAUL

Why not?

ANNE

Richard got so sick on it there I had to take him to the men's room. God, they write funny things on men's-room walls.

PAUL

(Annoyed)

The Village crowd is quite literary. Will you please let me pick my own dinner?

ANNE

Yes, sir. Just don't have the piccata.

PAUL

I'll have pasta.

ANNE

Good choice.

PAUL

Then a stroll through Washington Square Park. It'll be dark. Nobody'll see us.

ANNE

(Kidding)
We'll get mugged.

PAUL

Then, after the mugging, on to the Hotel Albert . . .

ANNE

Which leaves us about twenty minutes. I've got to be home by midnight or Richard gets hysterical.

PAUL

For Christ's sake . . .

ANNE

(Apologetically)
You *have* to walk off your dinner?

PAUL

All right, right after the tortonis we'll run to the hotel.

ANNE

It doesn't sound very romantic, does it?

PAUL

No, not with Richard vomiting in the john, it doesn't!

ANNE

I'm sorry. I won't mention his name again.

PAUL

It would help.

ANNE

I'm sorry.

PAUL

Okay, forgiven.
  (Smiles)
Friday night . . . Oh, *Christ!*

ANNE

What's the matter?

PAUL

I can't meet you Friday night. My parents are coming to dinner.
I'd switch it but they're in from Florida . . .

ANNE

Okay. That's okay.

PAUL

  (Thinks)
Friday morning?

147

ANNE

In the morning? You want to have an affair in the morning?

PAUL

It's my last day of vacation.

ANNE

(Distastefully)
But in the morning?

PAUL

The afternoon, then?

ANNE

Okay. What time?

PAUL

One o'clock.

ANNE

I can't. I've got to put Alexa on the school car.

PAUL

Anne . . .

ANNE

I'm sorry, Paul. She's four and a half and it's a spooky age. If I don't put her on the car, she won't go. A little later, that's all. I'll put her on the car, get Richard's shirts and come right . . .

PAUL

I don't believe this! I'm supposed to be having an affair, instead I'm helping organize a household!

ANNE

Paul, I have to think of these things, I'm sorry. I'm a mother of two small children and I have a husband.

PAUL

Believe me, I know you do!
(ANNE doesn't answer. Petulantly)
All right. Friday, at one.

ANNE

Thirty.

PAUL

One-thirty. Hotel Albert. Lunch first.

ANNE

Fine.
(Pause. They smile)

PAUL

Tell me something. Was last night all right?

ANNE

Wonderful. How was it for you?

PAUL

A bit conservative maybe, but not without potential.

ANNE

You don't do all kinds of funny things, do you?

PAUL

Not so far, but I'm willing to try.

149

ANNE

I saw a movie once . . .

PAUL

So did I.

ANNE

I thought you didn't even read *Playboy*.

PAUL

Some guys at the office took me. Who took you?

ANNE

Rich . . .
            (Tries to cover her slip)
Friend. A very rich friend . . .

PAUL

Hello, Richard!

ANNE

Well, *I* didn't say it. You asked me!

PAUL

You went to a dirty movie with your husband.

ANNE

Who better? We didn't enjoy it, though. We thought . . .

PAUL

I don't want to know what you thought!

ANNE

I'm sorry. I don't mean to talk about him. It just slips out.

PAUL

Are you going to talk about him at the hotel, too?

ANNE

(Beat)

That's unfair.

PAUL

I'm sorry, but every time you mention his name it's like you don't know *I'm* here.

ANNE

(Disturbed)

I'm very sorry.

PAUL

I know, it's hard for me, too. But when we're together, there *is* no Richard and no Janet.

ANNE

I know it must be . . .

PAUL

At least I know that much about having an affair. That you have to forget who you are and where you're from. You have to just go with it. You have to. If I let myself think about Janet, I couldn't do it.

ANNE

You're right, you're right. There is no Richard.

151

PAUL

Right. There is no Richard and there is no Janet.

ANNE

There is no Richard.

PAUL

Right!

ANNE

There is no Richard.

PAUL

Right!

ANNE

There *is* a Richard.

PAUL

Anne . . .

ANNE

There really is. He's the one with the sagging pectorals, remember?

PAUL

Anne, you're going to kill it.

ANNE

You're right. You're right. I'm going to kill it.

PAUL

Shut up, just shut up Anne, before it's too late.

ANNE

Right. Right.

(She strides across the room)

If I could just shut up, everything would be all right. Shut up, Anne. Just shut up.

(She slaps her own face)

Just stop talking . . .

PAUL

Anne . . .

ANNE

(It bursts out of her)

Paul, I don't want to have an affair! Oh, you're right. I should have shut up.

(Beat)

I'm sorry, Paul. I'm sorry, but I can't go through with it. I wish I could, but I can't. I just can't. I can't have affairs, I guess. All I can have is marriages. That's the kind of person I am. Look, I'm already worrying about what you'll have for dinner on our tryst. Before we went to bed, I'd hang up your pants so they wouldn't get wrinkled. I can't have two marriages, Paul. There's only so much laundry I can carry.

(Beat)

Oh, Paul, I really do love you. But I love Richard, too. And he's where my life is.

PAUL

I know.

153

ANNE

Are you all right?

PAUL

Yeah.

ANNE

Do you forgive me?

PAUL

Of course I forgive you.

ANNE

It's true for you too, isn't it? Isn't Janet all you really care about? And your son?

PAUL

(A long pause. It is of course true)

Yes.

(Smiling, almost with relief)

Boy, we came pretty close, didn't we?

ANNE

I wouldn't have been much good at it anyway. You wouldn't want a lady who'd be saying her rosary after every kiss.

PAUL

Nah. All that clicking of beads is too distracting.

(Beat)

Why did last night happen?

ANNE

I don't know. That's something Richard and I will have to figure out.

154

PAUL

You're going to tell him?

ANNE

What we *did?* No. That would only hurt him. But I'm going to tell him how I feel. I don't think I've done that in a long time.

PAUL

Yeah, neither have I. No. I've already started. I'm getting a club chair.

(The front door opens and EDDIE and the PREGNANT WOMAN enter. EDDIE fixes the doorknob)

EDDIE

Que carajo pasara aqui con el doorknob? I don't know, we're having a lot of trouble with doorknobs lately.

(He looks at ANNE and PAUL, waiting for them to go. They just stand there)

Uh . . . this lady's taken the apartment.

ANNE

Oh. Well, we'll be leaving then.

(As the WOMAN chatters on, ANNE and PAUL stand there, looking at each other. They realize it is the last time they'll see each other)

WOMAN

Well, Eddie, the first thing I want done is the sink moved and whatever is smelling up the place cleaned out. And the stall shower is missing tiles. Let's see . . . the sink in the second bathroom takes forever to drain, but I suppose that can wait . . .

155

(She and EDDIE turn to look at ANNE and PAUL wondering why they haven't left)

. . . let me show you the leak, Eddie.

(They exit into bedrooms, staring back at ANNE and PAUL)

PAUL

(Puts on his coat)

Shall we go?

ANNE

You go first.

(Beat. Tenderly)
Thank you, Paul. Thanks for everything.

PAUL

Thank *you.*

ANNE

Someday, will I pick up a magazine and see a story by one more sensitive Jewish author?

PAUL

You never can tell.

(Pause. With immense difficulty)

See you.

(PAUL smiles, walks slowly to the door. Before leaving, he turns back to take a last look at her, then he kisses his hand and presses the kiss to the doorknob. He exits.

ANNE looks around the room, gathers her belongings,

putting on her coat. She puts her hand in her pocket and feels the orange peel.

The PREGNANT WOMAN enters in the bedroom hall looking at her. ANNE takes the orange peel from her pocket and drops it to the floor and exits, smiling)

THE END